PLOT
YOUR STORY
3 EASY WAYS

Chris Rogers

Plot Your Story 3 Easy Ways
Entire contents copyright © 2015 by Chris Rogers

For information: P.O. Box 1734, Hilltop Lakes TX 77871
First edition published 2015

Printed in the United States of America

This book is dedicated to
writers everywhere.

Books by Chris Rogers

NOVELS

Bitch Factor

Rage Factor

Chill Factor

Slice of Life

Emissary

Here Lies a Wicked Man

FICTION ANTHOLOGIES

Death Edge Tales: 7 Nail-Biting Stories of Suspense

Death Edge 2: 7 Bone-Chilling Stories of Suspense

Death Edge 3: 7 Teeth-Chattering Stories of Suspense

NONFICTION BOOKS

Goosing the Write Brain: A Storyteller's Toolkit

Stand at the Cross Roads: A True Story of an Imperfect Woman, an Uncertain Future, and A Mission that Would Change Lives Forever, with Hilda Hellums Baker

For the Love of Radio and Mexican Food, with Gary B. Stone

Contents

Grab Plot
Wherever You Can Get Hold of It

Some writers love plotting, some hate it. Some writers plot their story to the end in incremental detail, while others prefer to work "organically," letting the story unfold on the page as it unfolds in their mind.

I strongly believe that whatever works for you, do it.

On the other hand, if you've been "going to write" that story for years and can't seem to begin, or if you've started and can't get past the middle, then maybe you need to learn more about plotting.

The Write Brain is versatile enough to attack a story from any direction. Many of us start with characters, and the plot grows. Others start with a plot idea and create characters to carry out the plot.

My favorite way of working is to start with a situation, and the people involved in that situation. I'll write a scene or two, maybe ten to twenty pages, then I'm ready to create a *rough* plot so that I know where to go next.

I've had students, though, who resist plotting even when they're stuck. Plotting is hard work, compared to just sitting down at the keyboard and letting the words flow. For me, the result—which is knowing where the story is going so I can plop down anytime and simply write—is worth the time I spend on a plot.

Some of my "organic" students eventually come around to it, after having to cut huge chunks out of their story during tedious rewrites. Yet one of my all-time favorite mystery writers, Bill Crider, tells me he never plots a story in advance. Yet his stories are filled with energy, intrigue, humor, and never fail to engage me. If "organic" works for you, great.

Here's what I do know: plot is a four-letter word with teeth. After spending days, weeks or months writing "whatever feels right at the moment," an ill-defined story line can come back and bite you.

Even a memoir or autobiography needs plot to make it interesting to read. Plot defines where you'll spend more words dramatizing a part and where you'll summarize.

When an editor says your story "devolves" into a trivial or preposterous ending, plot failure is to blame. Maybe you plotted it carefully, but your plot was never strong from the beginning, or maybe you took off on a new idea at the middle. Maybe you didn't plot it at all. In any case, the rejection is devastating to your writer's ego.

Because plot is hard for so many writers to get their mind around, I've approached it in the following pages in three different ways. You'll see some repetition, because a good story invariably follows certain key points. You might gather all you need from one way of plotting or combine them to create your own unique plotting style. The way I tackle plot depends on the story I want to tell and its complexity.

Most important: if you have fun creating your plot, readers will likely have fun reading the finished story. Writing is personal and subjective. Writing is also hard work, so it pays to enjoy the process.

1

Plot: 12-Step Story Development

As writers, we must cultivate the skill of stepping back, mentally, to get a broad perspective on the whole story. At the same time, we must be able to focus in close on the details.

My term for this is "chunking." As you chunk down to specifics, your focus becomes tighter and tighter.

Many different story-writing tools exist to guide you step by step. You may want to read Christopher Vogler's book *The Writer's Journey,* if you haven't already, or Evan Marshall's *The Marshall Plan.* I've used both, and they do a fine job. Eventually, however, I needed a simpler process and developed one that I find useful.

Tools not rules.

My 12-Step Story Development method is generated through the hero's resistance to outside (or internal) forces. It conforms to three-act structure, which we are all familiar with from watching stage plays and movies.

First, let's look at the steps we'll follow:

Setup

1. Situation,
2. Characterization,
3. Opposition,
4. Separation.

Complications

5. Initiation,
6. Complication, Complication, Complication.
7. Information,
8. Complication, Complication, Complication.

Payoff

9. Resignation,
10. Reflection,
11. Resurrection,
12. Resolution.

Now here's each step in more detail:

1. **Situation: What is the situation *or event that thrusts your hero into action?***

   In the film, *Tootsie,* written by Larry Gelbart, Michael can't get a job. Being out of work at the outset, he is in action, trying for one part after another. During these opening scenes, we get full exposure to the situation: Michael has talent, determination, and persistence, but no one will hire him.

2. ***Characterization: What are the* unique character traits *your hero must draw on or overcome to deal with the situation?***

Michael's persistence and tremendous talent are the admirable traits that will pull him through, but he also is hard to get along with, a perfectionist who argues loudly and persistently when he believes he's right, and a womanizer. He treats his girlfriend badly and takes advantage of his female friends. To land a job, Michael must learn to get along, or at least to choose his battles. To grow as a person, he must confront his controversial nature and his chauvinism.

3. ***Opposition: What is the* opposing force *and how does your hero recognize this force?***

Michael's opposing force is all of Hollywood. More specifically, it is every director or producer who refuses to hire him. Even more specifically, his enemy is himself: his attitude keeps him from progressing as an actor. Michael recognizes Hollywood's power over him but refuses to admit his shortcomings in working with deadlines and cast members. He rails at his agent and lashes out at directors who turn him down.

4. ***Separation: What is the turning point decision that separates *your hero from all that has transpired to that point?***

When Michael's agent tells him, "No one will hire you," Michael accepts the challenge, making the decision that spins the story toward change. Now he leaves behind his former way of interacting with his nemesis, Hollywood producers, and forms a new strategy.

5. *Initiation: What specific incident initiates your hero into the new, unknown territory that must be explored?*

   To get a job, Michael dresses the part of a woman and applies for a job on a soap opera. It works. To be convincing in his new persona, he must perform as he never has before, literally *becoming* Dorothy, an invented personality that not only can act the role required but also can get along with the cast and hold a job.

6. *Complication, complication, complication: What are the complications and how do they intensify to force your hero into harder and harder decisions?*

   1) Michael is attracted to his costar. Julie, who knows Michael only as Dorothy and likes "her" as a friend. 2) The male costar, an aging Romeo, is attracted to Dorothy (unaware that she's a man) and persists in pursuing her as a sex object. 3) Julie's father is also attracted to Dorothy, and Julie likes the idea of her best friend and her father being an item. 4) Only Michael's roommate and his agent know that he's a man.

   Note: As you write, don't forget Dramatic Unit structure: 1) goal, 2) conflict, 3) reversal. With each complication, the attitude going into a scene should be positive or negative; going out the attitude is reversed; or, go in with a goal, engage in conflict, and end with disaster.

7. *Information: What information emerges at the midpoint to thrust your story toward further complications?*

   To avoid the sag that often happens in the middle of Act II, the midpoint of your story needs to be propped up. What key piece of information can you reveal here to reverse the hero's attitude, situation, or goal?

   At the midpoint of *Tootsie*, Michael realizes he loves Julie, and his new goal from that point on is to win her affection.

If you use "death" in the middle, remember that death can be literal or figurative. Michael's old way of dealing with women (using them, lying to them, discarding them) dies when he realizes his love for Julie is too deep to ignore.

8. *Complication, complication, complication.*

Is your character winning or losing? In the first half of Act II, Michael's career skyrockets. Despite the problem of amorous men chasing him, and his personal conflicts with cross-dressing and so forth, Michael is achieving his goal— to work as an actor in a major role. Then everything goes wrong.

As Dorothy, he becomes Julie's friend, but yearns to be much more. Julie's father proposes marriage to Dorothy. The soap opera's infatuated male lead howls words of love to Dorothy under Michael's window.

In your story, is the hero getting hammered by life in the first half, then things start working out? Or does your hero make progress in the first half only to have it all fall apart?

9. *Resignation: What final blow resigns your character to defeat?*

At the end of Act II, the hero reaches a brick wall. There seems to be no way out, no way to win, no way to solve the problem, to gain the object of desire, to conquer the enemy. At this blackest moment (*crisis*), where everything is either lost or threatened, the character resigns all hope. (In action-adventure, this may happen in the blink of an eye.)

Michael, dressed as Dorothy and bearing a gift, knocks on Julie's door, hoping to talk. Julie misunderstands, believing Dorothy wants a romantic lesbian relationship. Julie tells Dorothy she loves her as a friend but can't "love" her, and requests that Dorothy tell Julie's father why she can't marry him. Michael sees no way out. If he comes clean, revealing he's a man, he'll lose not only his job on the soap opera but also the respect of his coworkers—which he has come to value. His newly acquired fame as a Hollywood actor will be history.

10. *Reflection: What **new idea** or reflection **brings your hero out of resignation and back into the ring to fight?***

During the crisis, your hero must reflect on all that has gone wrong—but she cannot wallow long in despair. There's something to be said for dropping so low that the only way to go is up. The character must now rise out of resignation and take action. In other words, do something even if it's wrong. This is the step that leads ultimately to the climax showdown between the hero and the opposing force.

Michael, rejected by Julie, recognizes his impossible situation. In *Tootsie*, the path from crisis to climax, from resignation to resurrection, is short. In other stories, and in yours, it might take several scenes to build from the blackest moment to the final confrontation.

11. *Resurrection: What action does your hero take to rise from the pit of dejection and **resurrect the goal?***

This is the "payoff" promised in the setup of the opening scenes. This is where your hero must overcome negative character traits and draw on positive traits, showing new growth and understanding to face down the nemesis.

Michael has learned to respect and get along with the people he works with, so he chooses to reveal his deception in a manner that does not disrespect the other actors, the audience, or even the studio producers. He "unveils" Dorothy on the soap opera, live, but in such a manner that the studio saves face. Because Michael has overcome his negative character traits, he deserves to reach his #1 goal, and his career can now progress in his own name.

Julie, however, is furious at being deceived. Thus, Michael's #2 goal is still elusive.

12. ***What remains to be resolved?***

If subplots have not been wrapped up, now is the time. If questions are unanswered, now is the time. If you have explanations to make, now is the time. The audience needs to wind down from the intensity of the climax and glimpse a small piece of the future.

What will happen for your hero now that the big problem has been resolved, the big goal has been reached? Usually, you'll want to tie up the threads rapidly. Every story, however, is unique and you must be the judge of how much time to spend here. A suspense story generally needs a quick resolution, whereas a mainstream drama with multiple subplots might need a few more pages.

Michael, meets Julie on the street and gives a memorable speech that he would never have considered at the beginning of this movie. He shows that he has learned to value relationships. "I was a better man with you, as a woman, than I ever was with a woman as a man. I just have to learn to do it without the skirt."

As they walk away together, we glimpse their possible future. Will they live happily ever after? Who knows? But we do believe they'll give romance a chance.

Expect Epiphanies

My early plots are usually quite loose and fit on a single page. As I finish a chapter, I see further ahead and fill in more details. This flexibility allows me to take advantage of ideas that spring from the interaction of characters or their challenges.

In the paranormal novel I'm writing now, for example, I knew we'd sail to Grand Cayman to visit a shaman for healing, and I knew his ritual would have less than optimum results. My intention then was to move on, but after writing the scenes, I decided the shaman would agree to try a more powerful ritual aboard the ship. When I saw how nicely that ratcheted up the tension, I decided the shaman would stay with us for the next part of the journey.

Be open to unexpected twists even as you write.

2

Rising Action vs Saggy Middle

The 3-Act Story Structure holding most films and stage plays together will work for you time and again. It's ageless and fairly simple. Here are the basics, followed by the details:

Setup = Hero + Goal + Conflict + Turning Point Decision

Complications = One Darn Thing After Another + Death and Information in the Middle

Payoff = Crisis + Turning Point Decision + A New Burst of Determination + Climax + Resolution

Act I—Setup

The first act of your story has plenty going on. Rising action is practically built in as you introduce the hero, the situation and setting, the hero's goal, conflict, other important characters, and the inciting incident that sets the story in motion. At the end of the Setup your hero is energized to make the *turning point decision* that spins the story in a new direction.

Act II—Complications—Midpoint—and More Complications

Act II starts off strong. The hero's decision causes dominoes to fall and he frantically tries to set them right again, all the time reaching for the goal.

But Act II is generally twice as long as Act I or III. This is not a rule; it just seems to be the best balance for storytelling success. With so much space to fill, how do you avoid the dreaded "saggy middle" that comes from the author running out of steam? How do you keep the action rising?

Here are two ways to bolster your story at the midpoint. I like using both:

- Stephen J. Canell, novelist and creator of such TV dramas as *The A Team* and *The Rockford Files*, tells us to prop up the middle of the story with "new information."

- Chris Vogler, author of *The Writer's Journey*, tells us we need "death" in the middle, real or symbolic.

In *Cinderella, new information* arrives in the form of a fairy godmother, and Cinderella's former meekness *dies* as she asks for what she wants, to go to the ball. Having both death and new information in the middle is a good thing.

Often, as in *Tootsie*, your hero will seem to be making headway toward the goal for the first half of Act II, even while disaster strikes at every turn. Then, after the midpoint, everything that seemed right is now wrong, and for the second half, nothing the character does works out, until the blackest moment when all is lost.

Conversely, the hero (as in Cinderella) might try repeatedly but fail in the first half of Act II. Then at midpoint, new information provides new energy, and the goal suddenly seems within reach. Amazingly, and despite disasters, things are working out, until a sudden twist at the end of Act II sets the character back at "go" with nowhere to turn.

This is the *crisis*, the blackest moment, when the hero has no resources left and no way out. Let's look at *Tootsie again:*

Michael's demanding nature and stubborn temperament have antagonized every producer in Hollywood. We see him trying out for role after role and losing, until his agent insists no one will hire him. But Michael needs eight thousand dollars to produce and star in his friend's play, and he's willing to do whatever it takes to earn it. Whatever it takes" turns out to be cross-dressing and pretending to be a woman *(1ˢᵗ turning point decision).*

After Michael becomes Dorothy, he wins the part on the sitcom, becomes a hit, receives all the fame and monetary reward he's been fighting for during his career—it's great, even though everybody thinks he's a woman. After the midpoint, when he discovers he's in love with his costar, Julie, *(new information)* Michael's stubborn, womanizing attitude dies *(death in the middle).* But now Michael's wonderful new life begins to fall apart.

Cinderella, on the other hand, spends the first half of the story with life getting blacker and blacker. Having lost her father, she's in a terrible situation made worse by her hateful stepmother and stepsisters (the villains). Then in the last half of Act II, things turn in her favor. The most beautiful girl at the ball, Cinderella dances with the prince while her jealous stepsisters look helplessly on. Before twelve o'clock, she rushes home, leaving everyone mesmerized and wondering who she is. Life is wonderful.

In either case, the hero's winning streak must suddenly

turn south at the of Act II and head for the *crisis*, the most hopeless point in the story.

Act III—Payoff

At the depths of loss, the hero rallies and makes the *2nd turning point decision,* moving forward despite all odds against success. This decision propels the story toward the *climax*, which is the final face-off between hero and villain.

The *climax* is the important Dramatic Unit your entire story has been building toward and must be played out with more emotional impact than any scene that has gone before. Once the climax plays through and the outcome is known, the *resolution* reveals what happens after the climax and briefly hints at what's to come.

Both Plot and story structure are easier to see and understand in a simple tale such as *Cinderella*. Yet even in the most complicated spy story or paranormal thriller, the underlying plot is fairly simple.

Rising Action with No Wimping Out

It's absolutely imperative that the hero—not a helper or mentor—faces down the villain. Walt Disney, in his wisdom, gave this important scene more impact in the animated movie *Cinderella* than the originators of the fairy tale did. While the importance of having the hero and villain confront each other may seem obvious, novice writers as well as veterans are often guilty of weaseling out on this often tough-to-write Dramatic Unit.

As you plot your story, look constantly toward the climax and imagine it unfolding in dramatic conflict between your two opposing characters. Watch a few movie endings and think cinematically. Make the ending powerful.

Your opening pages invite readers into your story world. Rising action keeps them biting their nails, as one darn thing after another puts your hero in physical or emotional danger. The final pages provide a catharsis of sorts, allowing a reader to close the book feeling satisfied even when an ending isn't entirely "happily ever after."

Play it Backward

If you get stuck, try jumping to the end of the story. Think about how you want it to end and how you want the reader to feel about the ending.

If that sounds counter-intuitive, think about it this away: You want to go on a trip this summer.

1. First, you have to decide where to go. Let's say London.
2. Where will you stay. Hotel? Friend's house? B&B? Why?
3. How will you arrive in London? Plane? Boat? Train?
4. What unexpected event happens en route?
5. From where will you start your journey?
6. How do you get the tickets? On line? Win a contest?
7. Where do you get funds for the trip? Savings? Steal it?
8. Who is going with you? Friend? Spouse? Child? Pet?
9. Why must you take this person?
10. What special clothing or equipment will you need?
11. What unexpected event occurs while shopping for it?
12. Why did you choose London as a destination?
13. Who tries to stop you from going. Friend? Neighbor?
14. Why do you plan to travel *this* year? Is it unusual?
15. Where have you traveled in the past? What happened?
16. Who have you traveled with before? Why not again?
17. What are you afraid will happen if you go to London?
18. What are you afraid will happen if you don't go?
19. Who can you trust to talk this over before you commit?
20. Why not stay home and work around the house?

Do you get the idea? If you're writing a memoir, decide where in your life would be a great ending. Plot the scene and play your life backwards from there.

If you're writing fiction, decide whether the lovers get together or not, and why, or how the villain is caught: plot that ending. Then plot the scenes that occur just before the ending, when everything has gone wrong, then the scenes that show *why and how* everything went wrong. Keep backing up until you get to the point where you're stuck.

3

Plot in a Nutshell

The late Dwight Swain, in his excellent book *Techniques of the Selling Writer*, told us, *"A novel is merely a long story. A story begins with a change in the way things are or fear that change will not occur, and* [dramatically chronicles] *how a character deals with danger—physical, psychological, or whatever—inflicted by such change."*

Using Swain's direction, let's once again break down plot into simple but dramatic successive steps.

Setup:

- Begin with an idea that hooks you. Ideas are everywhere.

- Pinpoint the prize for which opposing characters are willing and ready to fight—murder, treasure, a missing child, honor ...

- Devise a central character who will take immediate aggressive action to win the prize.

- As Alfred Hitchcock once said, decide what your hero will need to do, then give your hero the knowledge, skills, and abilities to make success plausible.

- It's good if the reader can like and approve of the hero. But don't discount the lovable rascal, part hero, part villain. Feelings, not just greed or duty, should be the motivating force.

- Pick a moment that will plunge the character into exciting action, then open the starting gate.

Complications:

- Pit the hero against a worthy opponent. Remember: the hero's strength equals the villain's strength.

- Outline the dangerous step-by-step action your character must take in the face of unanticipated developments to solve the murder, find the treasure, or rescue the missing child.

- Use the Magic of 3—two attempts fail, then the next succeeds, or two succeed, building confidence, then the third fails.

- Use offense/defense—the villain strikes out, your hero responds brilliantly, or your hero strikes, and the villain cleverly defeats the effort.

- Consider various types of attack—straightforward, circling in from the side, or completely clandestine.

- At every encounter, ratchet up the tension. Vary the type of tension—emotional, physical, mental.

Payoff:

- Work out a satisfactory conclusion in which the character your reader wants to win wins. A climax needs an unanticipated twist:

- Someone thought to be dead is actually alive/or vice versa. The coins thought to be counterfeit are actually platinum. The child was not kidnapped but is hiding from the rescuer.

- Be sure to plant elements that make the twist plausible. And make sure the winner *deserves* to win.

Some writers struggle with plotting, while others get the plot down quickly and move on to the writing. Often the best plots can be scribbled on the back of an envelope. Try this "Nutshell" approach and see how it works for you.

28

PLOT

Your Time Has Come

If you haven't already begun, start right now projecting your story idea to its conclusion.

1.   How (by what skill, knowledge, trickery) does the hero achieve the goal or solve the problem?

2.   Who's helping the hero (allies) and who's throwing rocks (enemies)?

3.   What mounting hurdles must be overcome?

4.   What skills, knowledge and/or deception does the villain use to prevent a positive outcome?

5.   What new information, and/or death, occurs in the middle to spin the story in a new direction?

6.   What setback leads the hero to the *crisis*?

7.   What decision spins the story toward its *climax*?

8.   How and where do the hero and villain face off?

9.   What is the outcome? Happy? Bittersweet? Sad?

10.   What is hinted at for the future?

4

Lagniappe: A Little Extra

Novels, nonfiction memoirs, and stories of 4,000 words or more can be plotted using any of the methods above. I must confess, however, that when I write short stories, I rarely plot them at all. I invented a method that works for me every time.

I START with a twist. Yes, I know the twist is supposed to come at the end, but bear with me.

By starting with a twist on reality, you already have surprise and suspense built in. Then I keep twisting the story as it unfolds until I reach a final feeling of *aha!*

In my first prize-winning story, *Spare Change,* which was published in *Alfred Hitchcock's Mystery Magazine*, June 1995, I began with the concept that in a mystery we *expect* something might be stolen, but suppose instead something valuable appears where it shouldn't be.

Here's how it opens:

Spare Change

by Chris Rogers

The Jag don't belong here," Murley was saying, big belly grazing the side mirror as he faced the young cop. "Anybody could see that. Sticks out like a damn poodle at a dogfight."

Jeff Rickey leaned his fifteen-year-old body across the hood of the Chevy he was detailing to swipe at a nonexistent smudge on the polished windshield. He'd never witnessed a real life crime investigation before and didn't want to miss a word.

Officer Packet stooped, hands on uniformed thighs, to peer in the Jaguar's driver-side window. Careful, Jeff noticed, not to touch anything and spoil the chance of lifting latent fingerprints. Jeff liked that. It meant the officer had some experience at crime scenes, and maybe something could be learned from him.

"Answer me this," Murley said, meaty lips pooching in and out as he chewed on the stump of a carrot. He'd stopped smoking cigars, doctor's orders, but said he couldn't get through the day without something between his teeth. "Why would any sane human being steal an eight-year-old Dart and leave this spanking new Jag XJS in its place? Don't make sense."

—

From there, the story unfolds with one unexpected turn after another until the final twist at the end. Like my friend Bill Crider, I prefer to figure out where my short story is headed as I write it. This one, which is about 4,000 words long, was a winner in the 50th Anniversary Mystery Writers of America Short Story Competition in 1994. Today it can be found in *Death Edge Takes: 7 Nail-Biting Stories of Suspense.*

What people are saying about *Goosing the Write Brain: A Storyteller's Toolkit*

"... This book will not gather dust on your bookshelf because you'll keep it nearby at the ready to give practical answers to your questions or to help guide you through unfamiliar territory." - N. E. Brigman

"...one of those unexpected jewels that comes along all too infrequently. The text reinvigorates the experienced fiction writer, and also provides a wonderful guide map for the novice." - Jack Lyndon Thomas, author, *Lights on the Water/ Impressions in the Sand: A Motorcycling Odyssey*

"As an author of over eighty published short stories, essays and poems, I have read a lot of books on the craft of writing. This is by far the best ..." - Charlotte Jones, author

"This book will spur your creative juices... It will literally program your brain to produce the story you want to tell." - Roger Paulding, author, *Bought Off*

"...a great reference book with concrete examples that can improve dialogue, plot and structure ... and the almost countless other details that a writer needs to master. This is a keeper. " - Claudia Herring, author *His Master's Bride*

EMISSARY

When EMISSARY RUELL arrives aboard Air Force One, ADDISON HALE, returning from her first campaign speech for re-election, has no idea she's hosting an alien energy. Winning a second term is essential; her failure would send a message that neither women nor third-party candidates can be trusted to run the country. When VICE PRESIDENT ROLLINS is taken hostage in Kuhndu, Africa, Hale must focus on the crisis.

Ruell seizes this opportunity to demonstrate one of his two bargaining currencies, the skill for non-violent resolution; but his attempts fail miserably, and his presence causes extreme physical stress. Desperate to fulfill his mission but forced to relocate, he chooses Hale's adversary, General Sef Yaqob, newly self-appointed ruler of Kuhndu—and prays his people are not doomed.

What people are saying:

"Rogers writes with confidence and authority about everything from African politics to Houston police procedure to Mexican drug gangs. There's plenty of action, and the book is populated with interesting characters from political figures to tattoo artists. At the end, there are enough loose ends to ensure that Longshadow and Ruel will return, something that readers will

be looking forward to. **Check this one out when you're looking for a real slam-bang change of pace.**" -Bill Crider, author of the Dan Rhodes mystery series

"...a well-written, exciting adventure ... the whole storyline kept me interested. And all of the characters were great - I loved the way the author describes them. If you're into science fiction with some suspense and "mystery," this is definitely a book for you... - MegHan, the Gal in the Blue Mask

"You're going to love Ruell. I've read a lot of Chris Rogers' stories, and Emissary is one of her best. The star of the story is a spark of light named Ruell ... among the last batch of emissaries. The planet assigned to him is Earth. He's like an innocent abroad and, to me, this is the most engaging and endearing aspect of the story. After several failures and on the brink of giving up, Ruell ultimately takes up residence in the mind of the cop. The Odd Couple, in spades. Rogers portrays both characters so well that you can't help cheering for them. I dearly hope we'll see them again in another story by this excellent author." - John Oehler, author, Papyrus

"Emissary sticks with you like glue. I have never read a novel whose character gripped me like Ruell! Well. Perhaps Scarlet O'Hara! This novel is a must read!! " - Marcia Gerhardt

"The perfect read. I have read everything Chris has ever written...this is by far the best characters....the most intriguing story ...and the most unique of all her works. I LOVED it! Don't wait get it now and read it twice." - Cobweb

"Emissary is a poignant and artfully crafted science fiction story that examines what it means to be human and the nature of free will. Author Chris Rogers paints a vibrant tale of loss, hope, struggle, and finding redemption where you least expect it ....Ruell is an emissary, trained to merge his consciousness with a human host in the hopes of convincing humanity to offer his people sanctuary after their own planet was destroyed. He first merges with the president of the United States. But when that situation takes a turn for the worst he finds himself merged with an alcoholic cop named Kirk Longshadow. This is where the plot really takes off as the developing relationship between Ruell and Kirk is the best part of the story." - Julie Ann Dawson, New Jersey

"... I even recommended it to my husband ... Chris writes a man's point of view extremely well (for a woman): no nonsense, straightforward. ... I particularly enjoyed some of the phrases she used when writing alien Ruell's thoughts, e.g., he referred to an elevator as a "vertical transport cubicle." ... I wanted to read WAY MORE about Ruell's world, his life experiences, etc., and I'm hoping her creativity blooms such that there is WAY MORE of that stuff in the sequel (a good cliffhanger sets that up nicely at the end). I think this book would make a good movie! " - Jeanne Purdue,

"Good book! Didn't want to stop reading it. Can't wait to order more by this author." Dorothy June Johnson

"While it took me awhile to really get with the story, the more I read, the more interesting it became. Emissary offers quite a combination of science-fiction, intertwined with what could certainly be reality, a brief comparison to historical events, along with mystery and humor. This was a thriller that I did not want to stop reading. If you want a taste of something different and enjoyable, you will love this book!" - Judy Thomson

"As soon as I read the description for the audiobook, I knew it was something I would love to hear. I was correct, I thought the story was incredibly intriguing, grounded in the near future in a very believable way. The characters largely felt like actual people, especially the two main characters, Hale and Longshadow ... the narration in this book ... went above and beyond, and made me want to listen to more ..." - Jeff F

"Addison Hale, Madam President of the United States, has

started her re-election campaign. *The sunbeam that glints off the rim of her teacup is actually Ruell, a biological energy spark from the planet of Szhen. Every being on Szhen has been compelled to leave the dying planet before it is too late. But where can they go? Chris Rogers opens an intriguing new world to readers of science fiction and cross-genre thrillers. As far out as it seems, she has made an alien entity a friend. We move out of our routine existence, reach beyond our mind's eye and enter her imagination. She has written a science fiction adventure that convinces you this could really happen.*" - JoAn Watson Martin, The Baytown Sun, February 8, 2015

"A well-written political thriller, with lots of action, danger and adrenaline. Laid neatly on top is a science fiction story of first encounter ... I couldn't put it down and I'm ready to buy the next one today!" - Tim Wolfe, *NetGally Review*

Emissary is published by Chart House Press, LLC

http://charthousepress.com/

Coming in March 2015

From Chart House Press, LLC

http://charthousepress.com/

About the Author

Chris Rogers

Chris Rogers was born in Texas and raised in the days of EC Comics and "B" horror flicks that could chill you down to your funny bones. She resides in a small community within commute of the four major Texas metropolises, where she ghostwrites business books and memoirs while turning out her own novels and short stories. Chris has taught mystery writing at the Rice University School of Continuing Studies, the University of Houston and in private master classes. Her students have received numerous awards and acknowledgements for their works.

After a career in graphic design, Chris became a writer the easy way: She read voraciously and filled blank pages with drivel until her fingers cramped and her brain defected. Eventually, she learned to craft a decipherable sentence. Author of the Dixie Flannigan series, *Bitch Factor, Rage Factor, Chill Factor* and *Slice of Life*, Chris has published stories and essays in, among others, *Alfred Hitchcock Mystery Magazine* and *Writer's Digest*.

www.ingramcontent.com/pod-product-compliance
Lightning Source LLC
Chambersburg PA
CBHW070510290526
45790CB00003B/1169